Weeping Willow's Wish

Written by Brenda Lee Elzin

Illustrated by Jana Borja

Weeping Willow's Wish

iUniverse books may be ordered through booksellers or by contacting:

iUniverse
1663 Liberty Drive
Bloomington, IN 47403
www.iuniverse.com
1-800-Authors (1-800-288-4677)

Because of the dynamic nature of the Internet, any web addresses or links contained in this book may have changed since publication and may no longer be valid. The views expressed in this work are solely those of the author and do not necessarily reflect the views of the publisher, and the publisher hereby disclaims any responsibility for them.

ISBN: 978-1-5320-8963-3 (sc)
ISBN: 978-1-5320-8965-7 (hc)
ISBN: 978-1-5320-8964-0 (e)

Library of Congress Control Number: 2019919542

Print information available on the last page.

iUniverse rev. date: 12/09/2019

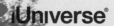

Dedication

For my son, John David, and my husband, John Sr. for showing me how to live well on our autistic journeys. And for my children, Cory and Caitlin, both of whom I am very proud.

The day the magic happened was a lovely spring day with beautiful new flowers bursting with color, fluffy little white clouds in a bright blue sky and a gentle stream running along its course, making pleasant gurgling sounds.

Willow trees stood along the banks of the stream. Their long thin branches drooping down towards the ground made them look so sad that they were called Weeping Willows. They were happy because they were different and special. But one tree in particular wished to be like other trees.

This one Weeping Willow wanted strong, stout, upright branches covered with large leaves that would change into beautiful orange, red and brown colors in the Autumn.

On this beautiful spring day, a large gray cat walked along the riverbank while her six kittens chased butterflies and tumbled playfully with each other.

They were having great fun when, all of a sudden, two of the kittens had gotten too close to the water's edge and slipped into the flowing stream!

Mama Cat became very alarmed and did not know how to save her kittens from the water. With each passing second, the two scared little kittens were being carried farther away from their Mama and sisters.

The sad Weeping Willow tree saw what was happening and knew just what to do.

The tree lowered its drooping branches and stretched them into the water and the two kittens desperately climbed onto a branch. They were not being swept down the stream now.

The Weeping Willow tree pulled its branches back to the river bank where Mama Cat was waiting. The kittens jumped off of the branches and scurried to their Mama, who was ever so grateful to have her kittens safe and sound on the ground.

Do you think the tree still wished to be changed to look like the other trees?

You may be surprised that the tree no longer was sad and embarrassed by its drooping branches. The tree did not want to be like the other trees.

The tree stood tall and proud because it had done such a remarkable thing with its branches that hang down toward the ground.

The tree now understood that every living thing has a purpose and that being different is so important.

Being able to provide shelter for the animals gave the tree great happiness and it loved itself exactly how it was.

In fact, ever since that magical day, the soft, gray flower buds that bloom every Spring are called catkins because they are a reminder of that wonderful day when the tree saved the kittens.

Birds and squirrels make their nests under the lovely drooping branches and rabbits make burrows in the shady safety under the tree.

To this day, the Willow's soft gray catkins reminds the tree that each of us have special abilities and gifts to share with others.

Printed in the United States
By Bookmasters